Vancouver Walking

Vancouver
Walking

MEREDITH QUARTERMAIN

NEWEST
PRESS

Library and Archives Canada Cataloguing in Publication
Quartermain, Meredith, 1950-
Vancouver walking / Meredith Quartermain.

Poems.
ISBN 1-896300-81-2

1. Vancouver (B.C.)—Poetry. 2. Vancouver (B.C.)—
History—Poetry. I. Title.

PS8583.U335V36 2005   C811'.6   C2004-906665-X

Cover and interior design: Ruth Linka
Cover images: Meredith Quartermain
Author photo: Karen Yearsley

 Canada Council   Conseil des Arts   Canadian   Patrimoine
for the Arts   du Canada   Heritage   canadien

NeWest Press acknowledges the support of the Canada Council for the Arts
and the Alberta Foundation for the Arts, and the Edmonton Arts Council
for our publishing program. We also acknowledge the financial support
of the Government of Canada through the Book Publishing Industry
Development Program (BPIDP) for our publishing activities.

NeWest Press
201–8540–109 Street
Edmonton, Alberta   T6G 1E6
(780) 432-9427
www.newestpress.com

NeWest Press is committed to protecting the environment and to the
responsible use of natural resources. This book is printed on
100% post-consumer recycled and ancient-forest-friendly paper.
For more information please visit www.oldgrowthfree.com.

1   2   3   4   5   08   07   06   05

PRINTED AND BOUND IN CANADA

for Peter

Contents

"Description is mystical. It's afterlife because it's life's reflection or reverse."

—*Lisa Robertson*

Vancouver Walking

Thanksgiving

a girl in Ontario dreams of an ocean
so large it cannot be dreamed—
                    years later
she's at the edge of the pacific

Gore Avenue—track of an old skid
        Surveyor General of British Columbia
            ran from a True Lagoon
                to a place between first and second narrows
the Spanish said people called Sasamat
            —no translation—
teals, widgeons, shovelers, buffleheads,
scoters, redheads, golden-eyes
blue herons and the *Branta canadensis*
        lagooned at Ka wah usks—Two Points Opposite
                sawmills, sewage, shacktown
till the railways paved it over.

                A skid from . . .
Chart-man Richards called it False—not a true creek
the Northwest Passage to Burrard Inlet
        for his *Plumper.*   To pierce or wound
run through with a word-spear   *GARrrrr*

Gore Avenue and Keefer Street
        iron palings
of Chau Luen tower. Boulders—
        hogsize—scraped up from an ice age
                Sit here.
Ice in the butt, face in the sun
till the shadow of Fan Towers South
                    slides across the page.

Steady foot traffic—east side of Gore—gaunt
                 black-leather-jacket longhairs—
down the skid to Hastings Street—lumbering swaggering
stuffing things in their jeans—gnarled man waving his fist
in, out, round and round his forearm—walking down
                                    to Lower Town

West Side. New Chong Lung Sea Foods
Crowds of shoppers. Shouts of the market men.
          A jade vendor and the lady who crochets hats
                 tucked in doorways/ cracks between buildings
                 their wares
People have lived here 10,000 years—
          Plump! a dozen fans open—brooms beating rugs
          Tai chi brush knee—
Cloud-ears pile up a wall—black and curly.
Sacks of dried mushrooms, dried fish and shrimp.
Red roasted seeds. Durian. Prickly fruit.
Barbecue duck and pork. Tanks of crabs, shell-fish.
                 A shiny fungus you see ledged out from trees
that clouds hear . . .

Round the corner to the wide Hastings Street
Captain Raymur's mill. Before that Stamp's.
"What is the meaning of this
                 aggregation of filth"—
barns of the mill, hodgepodge of lumber sheds,
slag-heaped bark, steam donkeys' rusted carcasses
scrapped blades and rubber belting—sawdust spit clogging the sea—
the mill-workers' dogs, chickens, shithouses, shacks—
Gassy Jack's saloon and hookers,
          Civilization's broken axes, saws, crockery,

junked bottles, tins, boots, shoes.
"DEATH to 'Merican freedom," Raymur said,
"I'll not permit a running sore to fasten itself . . ."

Brought the workers books, a place to learn.
Maybe even poetry or Dickens. Started Gastown's first school.
But named the mill for Rear-Admiral George Fowler H . . . ,
commander-in-chief of the vessel *Zealous.*

Round the corner to the wide Hastings Street
          Battle of 1066—
     Men lugging grubby rucksacks.
P U B (as in *p, u, b*). ATM Liquid Cash.
          Drink your money.   Here.
Mud-splattered windows and prison bars of the drug store—
before the Weald, a grab-bag of English infantry
     destitute of armour but for long-handled Danish axes—
the Normans on Telham Hill with central phalanx and two wings,
          archers, infantry, cavalry.
Hastings and Main. The Royal Bank. Pillars, bell-tower,
                         of Carnegie Library.
     People up and down the steps to the public toilets.

Hastings and Main. Four Corners. Fair lady works shuttles—
tripartite facade of the Ford Building—
     marble balustrades at its light-wells
     above Owl Drugs.
And the Four Corners Community Savings
     for welfare people, or what passes for wellness and fare.

Down Main to Georgia Street,
     not the Toronto Dominion towers

and terracotta fortress of Hudson's Bay Co.
    This is east Georgia—
hardware-shop barrel of stick-brooms
        where vats of white sheets and towels—
        the old Keefer Laundry—used to be
outside the law against Chinese washermen.

Rag man on a bicycle steers outrigger shopping-cart of rubbish.
Here's Keefer Bakery—window of bean cakes, almond cakes
Remember the melting ones
        like dinner plates from a hole in the wall on Pender.
Go in, the glass cases—clerks in red-striped bandanas—
        scowling. Yes!
Almond cookies, in packages—not cakes.
Do you have the melting ones like . . .
        like a memory of 30 years ago

Back at Gore—The Skid—bag of almond cookie in hand—
the giant redwood at Maclean Park—
who's made his home under it today
cross-legged near his cart of belongings.
He stands—barefoot—mounts a rusty bicycle,
rides it round through the gulls and pigeons,
and plastic bags.

Union street—they wanted to name Victory—
but didn't.

Crows in the birch trees
along Union
near the Lucky Rooms.
Crows in the birch trees—

6

"cakeshops in the Nevsky"
Sagging stoops, rags in dirty windows
           rowhouse on Jackson
Vancouver Improvement Company prominent shareholder

get the people out in the streets . . .
shoot the fear of God into them . . . they held back the bread . . .
the line formed at three, grew all morning
. . . all day . . . all night . . . Three days continuous. . . .
in the great square . . . an infantry officer commanded his men
to shoot. They would not. A student jeered.
The officer thrust him through.
And a Cossack drawing his sword as he rode through the crowd
                            cut the officer down.

                Bloodshed.

Thickened, clotted, dried cloth set into our garment.
Land cut in gore-shaped pieces
           to furnish with wedges
the flats Khahtsahlano called sk'wa chice—
deep hole in the bottom

        lake water bubbling up in the salt

        "cakeshops in the Nevsky" Pound thought
            in his cage at Pisa.

Walk to commercial drive

Freight train heading north to container docks,
                              grain silos, sugar factory
C.N. connector line
down the gulch where they shot ducks offa back porches
     in the tide-flood from the old lagoon

          Captain Raymur's street
               rusty chainlink corralling cable spools, pipe sections—
Earl's Industries welding steel—mops of rusty shavings
                    chucked in the skips.
          Pole dump at the telephone depot by the tracks

Git across on Hastings
          (cyclist to the traffic backed up at the crossing)
bridge over the gulch where the working girls hang
               inked out in the night
yellow flatbeds flanged wheels slow, then halt

commercial drive
          hacked out timber and stumps,
                    graded the bed pick and shovel
          barrowed the gravel—locked in ties
          $2 a day if white; $1 if Chinese

commercial drive
               Lytton Camp
          These fellows aren't working (Foreman)
They will do better (Chinese Bookman)
          No. Dismiss them from the crew.
Then pay them a quarter day.
          No. They are dismissed.
The timekeeper picked up a stone.

The workers grew boisterous . . . threatening
The timekeeper struck the bookman . . .
A teamster seized a pickhandle and waded in,
striking Chinamen right and left . . .
some of the Chinamen considerably injured
. . . one badly.

commercial drive
10 p.m. . . . a White rapped at the Chinese camp . . .
remaining a few minutes . . . he withdrew
and pretty soon the bookman saw 20
rushing down . . . all had sticks in their hands

Ripple of clunks, coupling to coupling—
        train goes into slo-mo. South.
Clang of the crossing lights. Flatbeds rolling back
        the way they came
Faster. Container sides wrinkling the alphabet—
yellow letters, orange blocks: Yang Ming
        The Y M Line   Harjin
        Tex   Flatbeds double-decked.

commercial drive
Mister Corbould, soon to be Member of Parliament—
        buy for $200, sell for $20,000—
                the Road's coming
6,458 acres Granted Gifted Bestowed Signed over Ceded to
        the Canadian Pacific Railway Company.
        For 12 miles of track.
As in corporation—artificial person—created at law
        with continuous existence, powers, and liabilities
                to make profits

5800 acres for Shaughnessy, 480 downtown
to Donald Smith—Lord Strathcona,
and Richard Angus, C.P.R. Directors
at the special request of the Board . . .
Witnessed: Lieutenant-Governor Clement Cornwall.
Signed: William Smithe, Chief Potlatcher, the Great
Commissioner of Lands and Works
for the use of the said Donald A. Smith and Richard B. Angus,
their heirs and assigns, forever. Amen

The said land
with 25 million other acres of good quality free of tax
and 25 million dollars
to the C.P.R. to Build, Construct, Assemble, Fabricate
The Last Spike
The Canadian West,
Van Horne's Road, The Great Highway from Europe to China,
Sandford Fleming's Ocean to Ocean, The Great Dominion
Steel
of Empire,

Wealth, jobs for all,
a Great War to end all wars

And still taxpayer dollars hired a Yankee contractor
to lay the tracks of

Civiliz-A-SHUN

The Marquis Donald Smith Strathcona,
Premier Smithe, His Lordship Montague Drake, Premier Robson
editor of the *Daily British Colonist*

                    busying themselves naming the forest
streets
with terminal city

commercial drive
Engine five-five-20 and the seven-oh-63—
        spewing diesel—goading the train
        600 Chinese killed in the Fraser Canyon—
            landslides, careless dynamite,
                scurvy and meagre tents—
300 corpses along the banks of the Fraser and Thompson
    sent to China for proper burial

Cross the tracks, herd of cyclists and highschool kids
                    going west
Run quick. The train's back
lumbering north for the docks—lickety split

        Harjin—Tex—The Y M Line
corrugated steel boxes—Cosco—Cosco—Cosco
        grease-caked springs and couplings

Premier Smithe: "It shall be unlawful for any Chinese
to come into British Columbia, or any part thereof.
Any Chinese who hereafter shall come into British Columbia
shall forfeit and pay the sum of fifty dollars . . ."

Then a hundred, then five hundred

Union Street and Vernon's drive—
Scarlet creeper twining up a telephone pole
at the Happy Planet juice factory.

           Forbes George V . . . Officer,
           Her Majesty's British Army
came to B.C. to make money in silver mines.
Ranches. Real estate and railways.

War's another potlatch
Which would you rather give away—
beautiful blankets, bowls, baskets
someone else's home-land,
or smashed cities, people's lives

Commercial Drive
man with silver hair at Norman's Fruit & Salad
smiling, running his hand over a long English
                    cucumber.
Young man with movable yardsale on the pavement
20 CDs, 10 pocket books, a pair of pants

Plump woman setting herself up
on the concrete at Third Ave
near a line-up on the city bench—
cups, tins, hats at the ready—
          guy comin' at her:
Don't be stupid, man. Back off. Don't be stupid

White car at a stop sign, Hey man, I got knives
I got knives, I got knives.

Commercial Drive
late-day shadows of petty store-fronts
man sweeping little leaves that will not leave

                        the pavement
worn-out trousers, grey T-shirt once white,
eyes down on the walk
Not a waiter—maybe a dishwasher
or was he someone who'd begged to sweep?

What you see

        is what

    Bull—life size brass, and well hung
        prominent Brockville lawyer
            Richards Street—Upper Canada
the Market

          and Georgia, home of the Bay

    Here Before Christ
    trading furs in
        Company Canuck

          carpet-bagger Albert Norton R . . .
    '74—blew in from the east
'76—appointed Lieutenant Governor

    the balls revolving
    raise levers
    closing valves

        of a steam engine
        Burrard Bridge-house—men's heads
in wigs on the prows of longboats
        —row of lions barking at the cars

        Sir Harry RN—pal of Vancouver's
not a Nightingale
        a red tile roof—Art Deco hint of battlements

        did not mutiny in Napoleonic Wars
thus Admiral

Mining B.C.'s number-two industry
a brick school house

Arbutus Street
            Archibald—botanist and naval officer
    menziesii
the fake half-timber effect
            ate porridge on Vancouver's ship
            collected seeds, brought home
the Monkey Puzzle

        just reached the beach and melted
            a month at Nootka Sound
    to this day has no pitch

    Balsam, Larch, Trafalgar following Point Grey
the lower jaw of the mouth of the land
        Sixteenth Earl of Derby—the tongue

            awash in English Bay
    and Sir Harry's inlet
            opened on her by revolted ships

    Captain George
                Grey
                Vancouver

died on board the victory
        the nose, the mental protuberance
        of land the Squamish called Ulksen

            lovers' hands

                    in each other's hip pockets
          at Skwàyoos
     walking backwards
                    as though the First People hadn't lived here
a thousand years

               hedges of laurel and cedar. Freighters
     secretary of the treasury
                    every man will do his duty

          inside
          the head or entering inland
               a *Secretum* with pigeonholes
he hoisted the signal

     a stenographer for
     Sens,
     Stó:lō meant woman-rock

                         Go to Chelxwàelch: dry at low tide
               Go to Pàpiyeq
                    at the tip (the bent end)

          Lord Stanley graphing his tongue
     what is narrow

          with freighters,
they are low in the water
                    past the rich houses

construction ahead
               sinks the soccer pitch at Connaught Park

                    Queen Vicky's favorite
                    I am the queen's representative, I am
            Commander in Chief
                    of the Canadian contingent
in this Great War

        salmon streams seeking the sea
still running at Tatlow
                    married the daughter
                    of C.P.R. honcho, a fortune in real estate

        Balaclava—Lord Lucan's slip-up
            The Charge of the Light Brigade
                    nothing to do with Edison's bulbs

        a battery in front—can their glory fade?

construction ahead, black letters, orange board,
            man and shovel
            built bridge at Spuzzum,
                    then the Cariboo Wagon Road

        Joseph William Trutch, Sir
            age 45, first lieutenant governor
damned if *he* wanted democracy

                construction ahead, temporary
the village of Blenheim on the Danube
                under the Duke of Marlborough and Prince Eugene
        always had a pack in his breast pocket

                after his wife died,

                    and his wife
                    and his wife
                    and his
                    and his
                    and his

            for the roundup   Home on the Range
                    52,000 English, Germans, Dutch and Danes
                    versus 55,000 French and Bavarians

        Waterloo—commenced at about 11:30, don'tcha know,
                the British lost 22 thousand, the French 35

                        trolley-wired day, architect of our networks

                        be prepared to stop
            a Dalmatian on lead
                            watch him defecate

                        Bank of Montreal in gold letters
President
            First Baron Mount Stephen

                        and the Jericho Garrison
            parleyed the contract for the Road

                        25 million acres tax free in perpetuity

    Go to place of cutting bullrushes
    Go to many-people-died container
    Go to bank-caving-in
    to greasy mouth

talk about your king of Gideon
          talk about your man of Saul
resourceful and cool, he never lost faith

          the wheels in a chair spoke
Buy Low Foods   take a Muffin Break
     car goes by vroom, then another one vroom, then another
                                                  vroom

          And they utterly destroyed all that was

only the silver and gold,
and the vessels of brass and iron
they put into the treasury
of the house of the Lord.

19

Walk for beans

head out across Campbell
          he owned the sawmill with Heatley
     after Captain Stamp died in 1872

head out
to the Russian People's Home
          cement-block hall—no windows
     a home away from home
               what was home under Stolypin:
          only themselves to hitch to plows
                    taxes and rent at 93 percent
        dung walls and dirt floor to share with pigs
pay the squires for water

               god is in each of us
     the doukhobors said, the "spirit wrestlers,"
                    Tolstoy helped 7400 head out
                        in 1889
                        in cattle boats.

1911 no harvest, 1912 starvation
          Kokovtsov barred the charity groups
               the foreign-owned Lena Company
        shot and killed 162 workers
           striking for enough to eat

head through the Raymur housing projects
          brick barracks yellow and blue walls
              à la public swimming pool
     in small-town Canada
                  pink metal railings broken blinds

    1914 Popularity and Flags

1922 Misery and Rags
              the vets said
shacks floats tents along the foreshore
              mezzanines, cellars
rooms with no window, light, air
       rooms 20 x 13 x 10
              for six Chinese single men
       LAUNDRY (sign on a plank at a door)
REPAIRING NEATLY DONE
       25 people per toilet
              no bath, no shower

       the rain came down in sheets
       I saw the legs of a man disappear
       under a pile of rails
       I stooped down
       saw what seemed to be men
       sheltering there—
       are there any soldiers
       yes
       a bugler in Princess Patricia's
       Canadian Light Infantry
       13 more under the rails
       2 without boots

Prior Street Jungle: crates, tar paper, corrugated iron,
barrels, tea boxes
       old Ford cars
              made trails called Granville, Main and Hastings Streets
       water from a gas station
       one privy, 400 men
              Relief Officer H. W. Cooper issuing 879
bed tickets for Pender Street refuge and

21

the old automobile building, Hastings Park

        for two weeks
    they stayed

Captain Raymur's Avenue
            with that ready business manner
        and in a beauty class he'd have his place:
            he said *death to 'Merican freedom*
    lawlessness
                what Judge Begbie was to B.C.,
        he'd be to Gastown

head out of the logos
        stand on tracks to stop trains
                    with the militant mothers of Raymur:
        Give us a footbridge to Lord Seymour's school
                type wrought in metal

the poem walks through turquoise chainlink
        "a half alien, restless population, ill at ease with itself"
                (Seymour to Buckingham, 1867)
walks over the tracks—the capital controversy

            arrived on her majesty's ship *Forward*
                    booming her guns seven miles down the river
            at *imperial stump field*
        "frail slight completely bald,"
        he saw
        "sky water eternal timber"

the frontier the idea of shape
                    course
                  meaning
                drops off a cliff
                or a cheek

          Court House: log walls (the logos) and canvas roof
      Royal City: the streets blocked up with fallen trees
            he built a ballroom for 200 at Government House
    supper rooms, furnished apartments, "viands of the most *recherché*"
        and the chain-gang to beautify the grounds

        welding as surely as Earl's Industries
    forges steel contraption on a wagon for
            Port of Seattle

    clamps hoists rusted metal slabs   heaps of black slaggy dust
                                    of machined metal
            giant curly-kates of steel shavings in the trash skips
    sheet-iron cut like butter
            like mother's dress patterns

                someone's strung up oranges in the bare branches
            across from Lord Seymour

        at *sobranyas*, Doukhobors sang hymns and songs
            to make the Living
    Book

Clark Drive zebra walk
            related to the horse and the ass
            look sharp like them, *watchful swift*
            difficult to capture. It is, however, much hunted

23

and seems destined to extinction
                    The Century in 1889

why drink coffee
we don't have to

        here on the frontier of where this is going

stopped at dumpsters, dead mattress and computer
        the drives, streets, avenues from history

        all thick forest
                when Israel Powell got it in 1877
                everywhere trees, underbrush
                        home to ravens bear deer
the sea invisible—sea-less
                now shorn skin down Victoria's drive to the grain silos
                        orange steel cranes gawking at blue-grey mountains
                the gate-way to the Pacific, they say

                to that which makes peace

if we could find it in the bricked-in ground,
hummocks of knuckle earth
                        down to the docks
        of containers

        old worn backs of the streets
        the art of speaking

a police cruiser's stopped
                lights flashing at Sir William Macdonald's School
        why don't they arrest *him*

he founded Macdonald Tobacco Co
    and the Macdonald Manual Training Movement
        with neither family nor frivolous tastes
    got the state to train hands for farm and factory

brush-cut officer questions two men
    of the first people—Squamish, Musqueam, Stó:lō—whites called
                                 Indian
        their faces, like their clothes, are worn, baggy
    seem gnarled with the war
    cross the street at the bus stop a sister watches,
                            angry, disgusted

    what has changed?
        since Stolypin's "agrarian question"
          the English Enclosure Acts
FOR THOSE WHOM WE MAKE POOR

Victoria and Hastings
    gas station, public school, Owl Drugs & Post Office
                  Sandwich Farm. Lattes.
      lunch counter tacked on the back of the building
anything you can sell to keep going

Lowertown 1920s
Rosa Pryor started her Chicken Inn:
I couldn't afford to buy but 2 chickens at a time—
I'd run my husband over there to buy the chicken
he'd just cut them up right quick
I'd wash them
get them on frying
I'd commence talking, "Oh, yes, yes, so and so and so,"
talk to take up some time

25

I'd see him come in, then I'd say,
"well, I must get those chickens on."
I'd get him to pay
say to my husband "Now, you get 2 more"

down Victoria's drive
                   a red-bricked hill in Her Majesty's
    red-bricked streets
        trains clang at the level crossing
  grain silos on the docks ooze aroma of barns
        chicken houses
        kid filling a galvanized metal feeder
                hanging over feather fluffs
                and balls of shit

down through the auto repair joints
    the rain-wrinkled plywood walls of warehouses

down to Powell Street, Israel "Wood" P . . .–
        arrived 1862
        1863 elected M.L.A., practiced his medicine
           got into the education biz
John A. made him Canada's first Superintendent of Indian Affairs
          he stayed for 17 years
        "you know, we really oughtta give them 40 acres
instead of just 20 for ranching   after all, the whites get 320"
        Premier Smithe let him in on the Road coming
sold land to Crease and others 1883 speculating
        bought some more from Campbell and Heatley 1884
made a bundle

        khupkhahpay'ay, the Squamish called that place
        on the shore of our now Vancouver

Cedar Tree
No, I don't want to *see them*,
he said in 1875 *when a question of such vital import*
as that concerning the quantity of land to be reserved for
their benefit
remains in doubt

I was glad to visit the Kwahkewlths in a ship of war ... (1883)
a proper show of authority is necessary
when endeavouring to break up their demoralising customs

the potlach, patlach, potlack
Tamawawas Gamanawas, whatever you call them

barbaric medicine feasts, the doctor said

Indian children so irregular ...
add to this, the vicious allurements
incident to the daily return
of the child from school to uncivilized camp life

The only scheme for meeting the difficulty ...
two or three industrial boarding schools
separated from native customs and modes of living

the coffee shop: roasters, sacks of beans
funnels, chutes, wire mesh—
rakes to keep the beans moving
over the heat

photographs on the wall
rooms full of dark-skinned women
at walled desks heaped with beans

picking them over

here they cost 12 dollars a pound
what did they get there

outside again, corner of Victoria and Powell
grey brick Hamilton Building and the Princeton Hotel
                              dock side
Colour Photo and the coffee shop landside
steady roar of traffic rushing toward town
or the iron workers' bridge
        crazyman—gray hair flying out
screams, points up Victoria Drive

            RIGHT HERE! RIGHT HERE!
points down at the pavement middle of Powell Street
                raging yelling
        oblivious to honks and screeches

out of the Hamilton Building comes a woman
six and some feet tall
            green velvet dress
enormous belly
        breasts splayed out on top
                steers down Powell like a freighter

        stops to gaze at crazyman
            moves on
crossing Victoria
        to the Princeton

Frances Street–

how many have walked it?

boxed against coastal mountains
Loyale Automotive, Winner Sportswear, New Profession Collision
       six blocks–
real-estate-man slash Land Commissioner
             Forbes George Vernon's
     up to Queen Vicky's drive

          the columned porches and clapboard,
                       classic   1905
               Sister Frances at St. Luke's
     torn down for Turbocharger Service Centre,
     Pacific Plating Bumper Exchange & Custom Chroming

     no person shall destroy desecrate deface
     no person shall demolish a building or structure
the facade
     the unsolved eastern question

Lord Aberdeen, 4th Earl of,
needed a hell of a lot of men
for Russell and Palmerston's war
     can't have Russkis owning Bethlehem

     maybe it's just one army or another
we're writing for the sky
     to read like fungus writes
        maps for us we think its blindness

             diggers in Dunsmuir's pits
     $1.20 a ton

2700 pounds on his scales
or maybe a dollar if he thought coal was slumping
and he wasn't gonna make his $8 a ton profit
$3.00 a day, if he didn't cut you for rock
buy your powder from the Company
pay your own helper
no pay for bracing tunnels
              funny how Mine Inspectors never found
the Right Honourable Robert or the Right Honourable James
Dunsmuir
                    at fault   the Act—whose act?
                    said miners were responsible
              for the gas at Wellington's No. 6
                    she'd pop from sparks off the hammers
                    working on their bellies to breathe
              it was miners, the Act said, made her blow—
                  they brought out brothers cooked to crackling
              it was miners
      killed 11 in 1881, 65 in 1884, 23 in 1887,
      150 in 1888, 75, then 55 in 1901

      soldiers of Master   Touch Auto Body
      Win Sun   Produce
      Club 21 Sportswear
            marching on Frances Street
stone blocks, end to end, where the car tracks went
      stitched in to cobbles
              streetcars a bust in the 1890s

            time of the small pox
                    I wish you would send a tent of
                    some kind as some men was

sleeping in filthy cabins and
they are all burnt now they
have no place to sleep
          Park Road Quarantine 1888

more yellow flags than dominion ones July 1, 1892
                    house after house
     sent express wagons
     driver clanging his bell cleared a path
     to Coal Harbour   Deadman's Island

          the standard as to quantity is still to be undertaken
          if crowding is avoided . . . we would be prepared
          to permit a longer period (City Health Dept to
                              Rooming House)

a large airy room, 60 degrees Fahrenheit
     remove draperies, books, furniture
               (George H. Fox, *Practical Treatise on Smallpox*)
          cut hair and beard short
     give purgative of calomel and soda
               warm baths   sponge the face to cool fever
                    feed the patient gruel, eggs, broth, milk, jellies
                    small pieces of ice
on the raging lips tongue throat
               in cases of delirium, clean the rectum
                         an enema of soap and water
          introduce four to six ounces milk and brandy

fifty-eight percent die
hemorrhagic form, always
          the gut bleeds

31

scrub the sick room with carbolic soap
> solution: bichloride of mercury 1 to 500

bichloride of memory
fumigate with burning sulphur and formaldehyde gas

> > > Palmerston convulsing/ terrifying Europe
> > > dangerous imperious monster,
> > > > Queen Vicky said

> > for the glory of Ottoman power
> > > squashing *intrigues* of Afghanistan
> > trounced China at Chusan, bagged Hong Kong

five hours in the House yelling
> > > *civis romanus sum*
> > the arm of British government protects her subjects
> > > against injustice and wrong

THE ARMS
> wherever they are

Frances Street—

> > four miles of straw-sacks at Scutari

4000 soldiers lying in gore-stiff uniforms
> > packed into place for 1700   candles stuck
> > > in empty beer bottles
> open sewer under the floor
> > no water, no soap, no linen
> no forks, no knives
> > > four hours to serve a putrid meal

for soap, bandages, food, 2000 in Barrack Hospital
> > die

32

Brilliant Doors & Co
Anglo-Canadian Automotive Supply
Foo Hoo Enterprises

diakonia from the verb *diakonein* to minister or serve
St. Luke xxii 27: I am among you as he that serveth: *diakonon*
Romans xvi 1: Phebe our sister . . . a servant (*diakonos*)
    refuge to orphans, aged and sick

            to the Right Honourable millionaire
                for 75 miles of track,
            two million acres (one quarter Vancouver island)
            all mineral and timber rights
            and 750,000 dollars
            as per   the *Settlement Act*

            miners living in two-room shacks
funny how settlers couldn't get
            lots under the *Settlement Act*
                till the track went in
        and they had to pay Dunsmuir's price

            Dear Sir,
            Thank you very much for the letter
            and enclosed cheque I received
            from you in response to my application
            to the Mayor regarding the child
            I wanted placed out. We found a woman
            willing to take it and so,
            as you say,
            the first month
            is settled for.

Yours very truly
Frances
St. Luke's Home May 6 1889

Liprandi clearing Turks off the Vorontsov Ridge
    cavalry pound down on Balaklava
        to the charge of Dragoons, the Dragoon Guards
spear in the flanks of Russian masses
    five minutes mêlée: the charge done

    Calvary: place of skulls   broken up fled
        in slight entrenchments
            Lord Raglan wishes Cavalry
to advance rapidly   prevent the enemy carrying away
    the guns

Lord Lucan, Lord Cardigan: look, I don't know what this means

    twenty minutes
    250 men
    500 horses
but ten mounted men mustered at evening parade.

C'est magnifique, mais ce n'est pas la guerre.

    then what is the *guerre*
    the *feu d'enfer*, rifle-pits pushed out, White Works springing up
the stumps still smouldering from the fire of eighty-six—
to remember forest, look down a street called Woodland
    orange cranes, ding-dinging trains at container docks

        no person shall alter the facade

shut up, dad, or I'll send you to a home
      an almshouse for illegitimates, morons, deranged
cared for by vagrants and drunkards doing time at the workhouse
                next door
      not what she wanted at St. Luke's

      born the year Nightingale went to Scutari
          British navy family—a brother Admiral Byron—
married William Charles Redmond,
Royal Navy Reserves   Winnipeg

two sons: one died in infancy the other in infantry
      Festubert 1915

      a long illness in Winnipeg
grieving a loss? two losses?
            the will of J. H. Greaves rebuilt St. Luke's in 1924
son sent to school in England
          would give her a cottage at Pasa Robles
      for healing
      archdeacon and Mrs. Pentreath
      life-long friends
but husband gone—where?
         she trained at Laval, Quebec
            deaconness and nurse

      Captain Knox, of the British expeditionary force 1759,
preferred the Quebec Hôtel-Dieu
      to his barracks' odious regimental medicine
         the Grey Nuns ran a brewery
      carted government freight
         to fund free hospitals, orphanages,

              nurses to homes of smallpox, scarlet fever, typhoid
canoed the rivers uncharted
        like Nightingale, she was of good family
she'd never end up in
        shacktown at the city dump

                        off Clark Drive
mufflers, tailpipes, paint drums, piles of old tires, coat hangers,
soggy cardboard cartons, bathroom sinks, garbage bags
spewing baloney wrappers, orange peels, rags

        you'll not see this on Dunsmuir Street's
                Duke of Connaught Regimental Drill Hall
                The Queen Elizabeth Theatre
                The Holy Rosary Cathedral
                The Institute of Technology
                towers of stockbrokers and forest corporations
for bodiless trees

                what's the syntax of
Frances Street
Dunsmuir Street
        the syntax of streets
                military plots   memorials to the missing

        the enemy relentlessly worn down
by exhaustion and loss
        reconnoitred gaps in the hedge

        "Say, Sam Slick, no dirty tricks,"

                yelled across No-man's land
hummocks, ravines, quarries, pit heads, mine-works
                even a pigsty
                        a Sevastapol

                seven hundred officers and sixteen thousand men paid
                        for six hundred yards

                workers outside the bumper and chrome place
striped cover-alls
                kicking a soccer ball
flies up
wedges in someone's roof-rack

                Sevastapol's battalions, squadrons, platoons
forming up
marching in columns guarded by skirmishers

infantry, cavalry, charges
                        enemy strong-points, trench positions

interdiction bombing: billets, stores, villages, railways
100,000 shells fired at the Jerries, May 13, Festubert
        half of them dead duds in the mud
                men armed with rifles worn out from shooting
or from the Boer war
        men armed with wooden ones:
                grab yr piece from a corpse, mate
yeh, that's the drill

                syntax launches a pincer attack
                        a bite and hold action

she placed a sanctuary lamp in St James
in memoriam

took in two boys
         named them for Scarborough Beach, Bowen Island
her home: Mark Beach, Luke Bowen
                              the breastwork defences
         built St. Luke's with Father Fiennes-Clinton
the town abuzz with stories of the fire
         Reverend Clinton, top of the mill-owner's house
                         throwin' on blankets and water
he rang the bell
         the two-room church jungled in giant stumps
edge of an ocean inlet   a church for boats to reach
                  rang the bell the fire melted
raging across false-fronted town from the downed forest's
stumps and burning

                  she brought them *socks shirts knives forks*
         tin baths cabbages carrots operating tables towels
soap combs for lice scissors bedpans and stump pillows
                     (Scutari 1854)

                  ordered 300 scrub brushes

               three bodies afterwards pulled from the church well
rebuilt St James on Gore Avenue, the old skid
and Oppenheimer the mayor's street,
         the one she asked for money to care
for a child *placed out*
for which he sent enough for one month

309 East Cordova (a.k.a. Oppenheimer)
46th Viceroy of Mexico
Don Antonio Bucareli y . . .
     why remember him?
     why not the province of Spain with its Guadalquivir?
where the peasantry not fully exploited
          are chiefly occupied in sheep-farming
and olives

The Vancouver Daily World
Christmas 1888 St Luke's: turkeys geese ducks
chickens confectionery fancy goods and cards for 16 patients
and those who could not partake in the joys
          and blessings of home

home run
     second base

        Boxing Day supper *the benevolence of Mrs. Salsbury*
     the square brick box of
        Patis Apartments still there
stuccoed over the only hint to their past
     the carved beams supporting the overhang
        1794 Frances Street at Salsbury Drive
            kitty corner to Wood's Grocery
thick forest to Sister Frances
     someone thought to photograph
     an example of early apartment blocks
     with small windows
on this street of bricks patched with asphalt
     vinyl-sided condos and low-rise rental blocks

        sugar-factory whistle goes   Salsbury
    runs down to
grain silos, cranes, container docks out-of-breath kids
      bouncing basket balls pass the red hydrant
talking of missing classes
    when did they lose them
condo-boxed neighbours yak balcony to balcony in January sun

> *nursing work as follows*
>   *confinements 37*
>   *operations 29*
>   *typhoid 11 one death*
>   *cancer 2 two deaths*

patient used to dig potatoes and vegetables
   from low swampy land and
roast and eat them several of the boys
   have typhoid

      patient moved into new house in Hastings East
  low ground   conditions unsanitary   flies

patient working at Ballantyne Pier

   patient camping at Whitecliff milk from small store
   water from river not boiled

patient over in North Vancouver drank from a creek

   patient living in shack foot of Cassiar
using well water   above C.P.R. tracks

patient looking for work at Chilliwack and Essondale

patient working in Harvest Field Saskatchewan
    place to place   *drinking well-water*

          patient working for C.P.R. on construction gangs
drinking-water   *an old tank*

    patient away from his rooms
for days   *drinking*

    Greyhound truck at Wood's Grocery
a man crawls up the hill on electric trike
        up Salsbury Mr. C.P.R. treasurer
William Ferriman S . . .
      a woman in flipflops and purple tent-dress lumbers in
    to Wood's Pepsi and lotto tickets
iron grate on the door slams
heads back nothing in hand
              scratch and win

        hills slippery with mud
    blankets of mist over the fields
        Soimanov opens fire at 7 a.m.
sweeps the British camp in Careenage Ravine

      General Pennefather pushes infantry
down the forward slope   Soimanov
breaks up his columns on the narrow ridge
            mist settles
everything in forty minutes
the whole Sevastopol column

41

expunged from the field
                    Soimanov killed
Pavlov attacks
            a sangar
                    the breastwork
        and the Sandbag Battery
the English carrying the new Enfield rifle
        300 yards   a sharp break in the slope
gives the assailants dead ground
        Cathcart's Division patches up the line
works along the steeper part of the eastern
                Russians descend   scatter it

        Cathcart killed

the front broken
                        cut off bands fight for life
            Russians seize the crest line, the sangar—
flung back to Quarry Ravine
                British siege train, 18-pr guns
                French horse-artillery
gallop down the forward slope
            1:30 p.m. by the clock they fire the final shots

Russians or someone, some thing
killed or wounded a third of the British

            a soldier's battle
                        Inkerman
            scarcely to be surpassed in modern history

the great need in the Home

is a new operating room
which will cost about $400

home economics

homogenized milk

$2,636.20 received for nursing services
24 cases nursed free of all charge

at the invitation of Sister Frances
the Nurses of the City Hospital
with their superintendent Miss Clendenning
and the private nurses of the City
assembled in St. Luke's Home
and went over in their own hospital uniforms
to the church and it was a striking sight
to see five pews filled with white capped
nurses

the day of the funeral of our
late beloved Queen

she took nursing
out of the hands of men   placed it squarely
with the Matron
        insisted on training
not intuition

Lord Dunsmuir of Craigdarroch Castle
    at Crocker's last spike
the Right Honourable Minister of Cabinet for British Columbia
in the *Portland News*: "he is rightly of the opinion that

43

it would be better for British Columbia
if it belonged to the United States
since all its natural commercial interests
are with this country."

> *if the bill would protect the life*
> *of one human being*
> *even a Chinaman or an Indian*
> *it's the duty of the Legislature*
> *to pass the measure* (R. Beaven, premier for 6 months)

> the miners safety committees say everything's fine
> nothing seems lacking
> everything's in excellent order
> a miner just used too much powder
> no need to amend the Act

"Bobbie the Boodler"
"A Cabinet Minister Abroad"
                    defeated the bill

*"heritage" means **of historic** . . . **significance***

a person who contravenes . . . commits an offence

"Chinese wages the only thing that makes mining pay"

$1.25 a day less fifty cents for head tax

"there have been not quite so many cases nursed as in past years
but they have been generally longer . . ." (1909)

"more cases nursed and more work done
                              than in any year before"
"our readers may remember what a very trying time
the past summer was for children": six died (1910)

"St. Luke's Home has completed its quarter of a century's work . . .
marked by the death of Archdeacon Pentreath, a firm and good friend,
. . . went to Pasa Robles, and as in the case of Father Clinton,
        died there . . . nursed by Sister Frances" (1913)

        homing in

pigeons   smart bombs

        "the Home has barely paid its way . . .
all over the Province"

                        *I'd be glad not to hire Chinamen
                        if the legislature would kindly amend the Act
                        to permit boys of 14 . . .*

"See the Conquering Hero Comes"
the Esquimalt and Nanaimo Railway: Washington's bridge to Alaska
        men unhitched the horses, dragged the carriage themselves

        *you want 10 cents a ton more
        I'll close the mines*

                *I would have argued for federal subsidies
                even if I wasn't the railway's major shareholder
                I haven't got nothing to hide*

45

visitors to St. Luke's 1907
        Lord Bishop of the Diocese
        Lord Bishop of Columbia
        The very Reverend Dean Paget
        The venerable Archdeacon Small
        Reverend J. Leech Porter and Mrs. L. Porter
        Sister Gertrude of St. John's Toronto
        Miss Rickards of Tokyo
        Miss Bernap of Portland
        Miss Pooley of the Korean Mission
        Miss Bridges of Surrey England
        Mrs. Ditcham of Lytton
        Miss Ellis of Carcross Yukon

        Moved by Rev. F Clinton
seconded by Miss Redmond
        that the seal the impression of which is affixed hereon
        shall be the corporate seal of the society (Nov. 18, 1903)

1907: selected her plot in Mountain View Cemetery
        25 years before she'd need it

        a complaint has been received by this department
regarding the above property

        it will be necessary for . . .
                the removal of all organic refuse

St. Luke's Day-Book October 1911

        maternity
        alcohol

curettement (op)
accident
alcohol
abscess (op)
typhoid
alcohol
alcohol
puerperal mania
alcohol
fractured patella
abscess (op)
pleurisy
neuralgia (died)
alcohol
nervous prostration

the miners were allowed to elect the gas committee
well Mottishaw and his partner found gas in some place
the company didn't like it and fired them

they had to flood the mine to get the bodies
every man was killed

Voysey, Charles Francis Annesley
first modern architect to design houses free of reminiscences
at 13 saw his father expelled from the church: he would not
subscribe
to the doctrine of everlasting hell

"Sister Frances has pleasure in announcing
St Luke's Home will be formally opened
Thursday, July 5th . . .

His Lordship the Mayor has kindly consented"

seven beds in a clapboard house
    half-timber under the peak
then fish-scales, three leaded windows across the front
canvas awnings   two nurses on the stoop

        rebuilt by Sharp and Thompson, 1924—Voysey's fairy tale
            earth hugging
            low walls below immense pitched roof
            Hansel-and-Gretel windows

        tucked in the city behind Clergy House
and the new St. James she never saw

        no fire'll get this one, Father Clinton,
with its eight-inch concrete walls
                                this cross
between medieval castle
            and modernist bunker

                St Agatha   *diaconia* at Rome
her glorious death
                Quintianus chopped off her breasts
                    for choosing Christ
over him

Father Clinton's St. Agatha's Chapel for his mother's birthday
                what possessions

        became her Guild

          for flowers on the high altar
for half a century

                a representative of **The World** looked in
          370 tons
          22 guns
          built as a collier
Cook called her
          Endeavour, His Majesty's Ship
          for the voyage to observe
          the transit of Venus

International Rooms

For Someone in Heart Surgery

walk along seawall
the edge of this
white frost encrusted sand
the shimmer the mirror of sea
the line of glass distance to sky
freighters rusted hulls stilled
a vast singing organ of day
of sunshine of bright logs
on the beach, of bright dogs
fetching sticks or a man's walk
on top of rock wall above waves
shading his eyes, water glimmers
his cheeks, forehead, lapping
sea at shore, the shore of this
gathering
flock of buffle-heads huddle
in shallows, diving, bobbing
up, shaking wings with squirps
and squinges, woman towed
by flock of terrier sniff at
grass and earth, an artist's
yellow loop encircling sky
sea, trees pull into this
skinhead youth burly sunbaked
between log and boulder
skateboard, wheels up,
on outstretched legs
shoulder tight to his mate
with dirty ball-cap on matted hair
jeans grubbed, torn, running shoes
worn through, a gnarled hand
holding a cup made of plastic,

whole crew of men jogging
office out for lunch of lycra legs
striped trainers, white socks
shirts black and red black
and blue, black and yellow
thudded bodies pound
past mother speaking French
to toddler ambling behind stroller
red cheeks, eyes blue as the sea
pull
pull into this
three white dots on black
feathers of ducktail
pull into this day.

Cochineal

A small fiery dome of black spots
crawls in my lamplight—
with tiny articulations
of edges of paper and
smooth blue plastic of pen.

Now and again she stretches her wings.

She holds paper surface
ridged with the fibres of trees
in her hands, or, if you like, her non-hands—
what we give insects for hands.

She comes to rest again
in a valley between two red hills,
facing away from the green felt
scalloped around a pinhead
of Remembrance Day poppy.
So jaunty on its straight-pin stalk—
its scarlet plastic is fuzzed
and puffed to undulate
like petals.

Under her fiery dotted back
she has tucked her legs,
or, if you like, her appendages,
that hold on to the rough poppy redness.
The whitish patches we might see as eyes
face the gray light from the window.

It is November. Would she like to go now
from my warm, dry desk to wet leaves and frost?

Will my book explain the desires of insects?
It does not list ladybugs.
Should I look in my index
under insects?

Ladybird beetle, they call her,
from the family Coccinellidae.
A dash of colour across my tongue—
a hummingbird from Emily Dickinson.

And when eyes are hummingbirds
who'll tie them,
with a lead string, Williams asked.

And when words
are humming
birds
who'll set them free?

"Ladybird, ladybird
fly away home, your house is on fire,
your children all gone."

Flash of wing-light zips from the scarlet poppy.
Gone? To my blue wall?
the bright quilt? the lamp? Ah—the black
plastic of telephone
passage to midnight sky
to the space in darkness.
She walks along, then headfirst down a vertical side,
then upside down the underside
to a keyhole

the telephone could hang on a screw-head.

On the tops of mountains in late summer,
the book says,
Ladybird beetles gather on rocks,
then crawl beneath
with friendly red bodies
for their winter sleep.

Can I call her this—
tell her this—
inside my telephone?

Night Walk

west on Keefer Street
past the dark park, the SRO house
heavy-metal whines from a window
to a husky on the porch
rows of bunkhouse doors
single-room occupants
some sunk below the street.

Chain-link fence at the schoolyard,
man pushes a shopping cart east—
plastic bag on head—bishop's mitre.
Through windows, men in their armchairs
with newspapers.
Turret house—its witch's hat
for the school's first principal—
snapped up by a landscape architect
his hostas and bananas,
white stars of Clematis.
On a bench, elderly Chinese—
one pushing the bench,
the other sitting. Talking.

Further on, Joy Mansion—
lo-rise cubicles for old folk,
bank of mail boxes,
brown carpet wall-to-wall.
Then Good Fortune Rooms,
dusty pipes and patched ceilings,
red-letter EXITS to skinny halls—
custodian lends you 10 bucks at 50%,
you don't pay, he'll rough you up good,
if you don't die of smack or crack.

Gore Avenue—north,
red and green awnings,
shops shuttered, barred.
Street-market trinketeers gone home.
City barricades still up.
Lichee nuts, gailan, durians
at the place on Keefer that's always open.
Pender Street, east, back of Strathcona School.
Shouts of boys holding hockey sticks—
revved up with the game.

Pender and Campbell Avenue—
the mill owner's street—
Sacred Heart,
its school and chain-link yard,
its rows of upper windows—
glass and bars—
single-roomer nuns or priests.

A grinding buzz—
the church's transformer—starts up
in the yellow dimness of street-lamps,
the blocks of housing for the poor.
A man scrapes along the sidewalk.
Muffled television thumps
over the asphalt
to the locked crossed doors.

First Night

bus to Point Grey the earl I type bust
through Chinatown it's free tonight along Pender Street
wheel chair gets on bus driver kicking the seats up
with his boot strapping the chair in chair-woman
accompanied by young man & folded scooter
young woman a man's over coat over her
shoulders they get off on Burrard Street
at the Ports store and the Royal Centre
the Vancouver Hotel all aglitter—we
carry on past St Paul's Hospital its star-shaped
strings its rainbow arches of lights Davie Street
a block later squeegie kid on his haunches
on a rim of asphalt at a gas station squeegie
and plastic pop bottle of water in the shadows
of a battered hedge he pulls his feet in closer his arms
fold tighter into the folded legs his hands make
fists on the tops of his knees and he bows his head
into the fists a small scrunched skeleton
in thin hood as though to sleep against the buses
and cars roaring past too fast to run out and clean
windshields for a loonie

on the way back in the first hour of the first
day a crowd on Point Grey smoking pot
hey there's the bus run for it Happy
New Year Happy New Year the bus
jammed with jolly people tiny pointed
hats rainbow coloured wands
a woman with pink hair another
with earrings flashing lights blue and red
all starry eyed crowds at Burrard's Bridge
the San Fiorenzo 42 guns no room no room

lights on the bows and wheelhouses of boats
at the wharves
Premier Smithe's attorney Davie street
someone in a blanket under a shop awning
no room no room till the Royal Centre
strangers hugging in the street youths high-
fiving it whooping yelling at the bus wheel-chair
woman the same one cannot get on no way
to know she cd've if she'd wheeled to the next
stop turn right on Pender past Malone's Pub
the Vancouver Vocational Institute
Tinseltown mall the Chinatown gate Asian man
working woman off shift get on ragged
haggard streetmen no parties
for them shops dark buildings of brick not
plate glass turn the corner at Gore the concrete
viaduct the warehouses for produce the small
dusty homes cheek by jowl on Prior
Edward Gawler shareholder Vancouver Improvement
Company chainlink fences around matchbox yards
I type years patched in porches and bare
lightbulbs clashing siding rickety steps
the poorer older the first Vancouver
that has not the means of tiffany lamps grand
pianos wide porches stone pillars
has not the means of
gardens and views
happy new year
it's free tonight

Cathedral

Holy Rosary gothic revival
Salvation Army stone, brick
Suzette's sandwiches
Cathedral Square
where coal-baron Dunsmuir
crosses carpet-bagger Richards—
men, boys, in cheap track-pants
slouch on benches under an arch
of scaffolding—
squeegie kid leans on its concrete pillar—
the night's street-light steely grey
face of a backpacker on the church steps.

Soup to salvation, General Booth said,
my soldiers are saved to save—
build shelters, hostels, farms, nurseries,
hospitals, half-way houses, language classes.
Volunteer work's what holds society together
(the premier in his government address
to the Army)—$2.7 billion worth a year.
In Victoria, we're going door-to-door
for $45,000. We've got 326 shelter beds.
And we're helping people with disabilities
find rewarding employment.

In the square the men trade hits or cigarettes
under a vaulting of stars.

Lucky Spider

thick-eyed drive
going where but
start over Maurice says
Odysseus to hell
to the barbarian other
on the back porch
it's a swallow
doesn't look it
it's thin, it's sleek
not a swallow
what then
no-name bird
all his weekend friends
he'd invited to the cottage,
in Limerick—roasted lamb, chicken
best vintage—next morning
cooked sausage, eggs, bacon
friends jolly never thinking
he 63 would drop dead
getting a wrench
from the boot of his car
the web between chair and table
busted shut shattered
for knives and forks—human stupidity
a star destined to explode
eons ago

spider scampers away
through the floor boards

Nightwalk on Ferguson Point

tangerine horizon
to Botticelli's duck-egg
and the new moon
a few feet over English Bay

slosh smack
sea sprays up
hits the wall
scatters water-pebbles

people on wheels glide in the shadows
past ducks lined up at the swimming pool
heads under wings—dark heron out
over silver surface the jiggling shuddering waves

past silhouettes of trees in three black clumps
on Ferguson Point, whiff of the drains,
a woman holds a child over the wall to pee—
"Andrew's abusing . . . " someone says, "he's abusing
his talent."

Spider's rebuilding his web

threads to the deck chair
the trellis, the late afternoon
and evening
suspended glimmering
the fiery green of Robinia
the lolling seed-cones of butterfly bush
a thin edge of moon

kiwi tendril up to the hydro wires
staff, score, rules for the birds
crisscrossing the sky
and the pocked pole
with its metal drum of PCBs
transforming the moon

Record,

that I picked up the trash can from the lane
      and put it back in the garage.
that there is a lane.
that it runs between houses on squared plots of land.
that garbage trucks empty trash cans—men driving—men
      picking up trash all day,
        5 days out of 7—their verve, their thoughts,
        their touch and smell, the universe
      of their eyes picking up trash

      so they can live on a rectangle in a house that's squared,
      and put out trash
      in their lanes.
that down the lane past the backs of other garages
      stands a shopping cart spilling rags,
      torn plastic, cardboard, a pink soggy blanket—
      parked at the lane-house door
      behind the car the lane-house man is constantly washing
      with a garden hose.
that there are lane-house men and garbage men.
that a red truck stood tipped on a hill of dirt in the park—
      dinky-toy yellow earthmover
      caterpillar climbing the fresh soil—scoop hooked up
      under its snout.
that we still believe in building parks.
that the wind swirled up the whole expanse of brown earth,
      and the flock of Canada geese
      had landed again looking in the park for an old lake.
that outside the show-mart, a man carrying a clipboard stepped
      out of a white van.
that men must drive vans, must deliver orders to match words,
      things to match numbers,

be good at this, feel important, and smile.
that a black and white jogger trotted past the big windows
    of juice bars and cafes on the sea-front, pushing a child-
    stroller—a new-fangled tricycle, baby lolling back in its
    hi-tech hammock, looking at sky or parent, looking up
    at highrises up to the clouds—it's hard
    to look at glass, concrete, like so many others,
    and not think the builder has made something of himself—
    and has he? Other than an erection—
    a jagged stalagmite for cliff birds—did he ever think of
    Christopher Wren
    or Homer—look at the highrise towers—
    what do they mean? How step outside them?
    Stalagmite peach-fuzz to the planet's pin-prick
    in the vast velvet of space.
that this is a string, not Chinese boxes, of memory—
    winding in, spieling out—yo-yo—
    on-coming cars stopping for cars turning left to Burrard
    Bridge—a signal-light red—
    they obey, that could easily disobey—operating cars,
    we are signaled—
    babies in strollers, and now, where's the switch?
    No it would not be death to wake up, see the signals,
    cross the bridge, the fact of the bridge, the fact of the city,
    men wanting a bridge, raising money to make bridging,
    damn the nay-sayers—a bridge to
    the idea of bridge—flow-thru smooth—no stopping of
    wagons, lugging of trunks to boats, rowing of boats,
    lugging of cartage to another wagon—in trunks of words,
    elephant snout, in, out—rather a river over the river—
    past the tax authority,
    past the brewery big as the stadium, tanks like oil silos

        making the beer of this
        trash pick-up, clipboards, car flow, people in their insect
        millions, their pimples of highrises, bridges, pyramids,
        and wars to crush other insect millions.
that the nametag on the gas-station man said Dick.
that he used a chrome gauge for air in the flat tire—phhhhht—
        32 pounds—phhhhht
        a pound extra—pounds of air in rubber on steel rims—
        slice it like bacon.
that a man on Homer Street stood staring at a shiny plastic tablet:
        billboard charity drive—loonies with grizzly bears
        for Air Canada.
that the public world is here.

September 11, 2002

brown-backed sparrow on the edge of a tin
Gloria's left for thirsty dogs outside the store
three men drinking coffee under the awning
sparrow dips her beak

inside, Andy, Gloria lean against the counter
facing away from the till
arguing in Portuguese

milk bottles down beside candies and gum
I slip between shelves of oil, tomatoes, pasta,
to the cooler

not to disturb their talk
their moment together without customers
in the 12-hour day of the 7-day week

"you're focussed on doing what you want,"
man says to his coffee buds, as I leave
"then you're happy—glorious"

INTERNATIONAL ROOMS

painted on the old bricks of the Arno Hotel

PUREST
OF ALL PURE
FOODS
CHRISTIE'S BISCUITS

The Arno door at 291 Union
bay windows over the produce and vegetable market
spilling out on the sidewalk

No Visitors after 11 p.m.
or before 9 a.m.

Enough Already!
If you can't abide by the
visitor rules
then STAY OUT

if everyone had an international room
would there be enough room on the bus

Please put mail thru stainless steel slot

Candid Camera,

you're in Canadian diner. Vancouver Street. West Coast. North
America. The World. A Universe. Writer pins on self with a tale.
From the donkey. Across the street, Books New and Used,
Travellers Inn, a detox centre.

Sit anywhere, the waitress says. December 17. Writer gets a
window seat in green vinyl booths, oblong mirrors, pastel walls.
Pots of green plastic plants. Red lampshades. Pepsi sign above
the hatch to the kitchen with its solitary cook, solitary waitress
out front. Faux Motown Supremes on the musak.

Chicken 'n Vegetables turns out to be mainly broccoli and
something that could be dog. Four ninety-five. So what's the
matter with dog? Rotweiler steak. Roulade de Pekinese. Could
be good.

Includes soup. Three other tables occupied. Old chrome servi-
ette dispensers. Chrome-top sugar shakers. Salt and peppers—
glass with plastic tops coated in dust.

Orange teapot, a band of carrots geese fish and mushrooms
marching around it. For tea? No. Soy sauce.

Canada $1,000,000 bill posted big behind glass coffee pots,
back of the counter and row of swivel chairs. Trolley bus stops
outside next to men with shopping carts of scrap metal.

Dog is edible. Like manikins in Sears. A pair of white arms on
the floor beside each white armless, nipple-less torso.

Single men for lunch. Older. Or business men at the lower end
of sales. Someone today scrunched into a notch on the outer

71

wall of London Drugs. Someone else (her coat was good) hunched over him.

A man at another green booth is moving the spoon round his cup very very slowly.

Backwards from Pender Lake

Starlings flock on the sidewalk to a man scattering seeds,
              bread bits,
   from his seat on an empty planter
on Keefer Street across from soccer fields fake turf
   a whole city block
       green like the grass of meat counters.

    On my back, pounds of books from the library—
the yellow pack that Maurice thought too touristy for Dublin.
Saw the starlings swarming the man,
       his grubby trousers and battered hat.
Before that, crossed Abbott Street—
       boss of the C.P.R., said
   No. I'm not putting gates at level crossings.

Met a man and a woman with garbage bags,
     green plastic—a few pop tins in the bottom
        they'd been picking.
   We kin go up say Hi to her
or we kin keep picketing, he said
     walking past Pender Lake chain-link,
       abandoned trailers of white hard-hats
    Concord Pacific's International Village—
land taken AGAIN from people—
     like Whoi-Whoi and Snauq from the Squamish
for a song.

No one's leasing at International Village—
     can't hack the rubbies, rummagers, cart people—
dealers hanging out, people shooting up
       in Andy Livingstone Park,
   Pender Lake and the soccer fields

                        indoor-outdoor carpet.

Livingstone.   commissioner of parks—
               Doctor, I presume
prescribed workfare in 1968.
      Let them build lawns, trees, rose gardens,
                        he said.
      The Board approved.

               The pickers or picketers, if only they could,
walked beside me—skeletons in yard-sale pants,
                        broken nylon zippers—
      green garbage bags of tins grubbed from trash bins.
Beside my yellow pack with its buckled straps and books
               where the tide came under Pender boardwalk
      before men who would swallow the sea
               held it back.

Pender Lake—a hole in the ground
               for a tower of stores and condos.
      On the side to the sea at False Creek—
               but what was true—
they drove huge steel plates in the ground—
               a rusted wall—a dam.
      It filled up anyway,
                        seeping in through the subsoil.
Water holed in—in a hold for ducks to swim.

Alders seeded, grew to saplings, even trees—
      a woods around greeny weedy water—
               fenced off from teeter totters and swings,
the concrete tangle of viaduct and transit tracks to and from the city.

I walked behind the picker picketers
then ahead past a skate boarder, a family of tourists—
        a boy and silver scooter wandering out
        the new Chinatown gate for sight-seers—
                dressed well in holiday ease,
spinning out the afternoon till the guide book's dinner.

Before the lake, the library, the concrete hillside of CBC—
        a man and a woman in jackets and leather shoes.
I wanta see all the Benzes, he said
                on familiar terms with them,
        like people who drive Beamers, not BMWs.
We crossed Georgia Street.
        The Strait George Vancouver called after the mad king.
                In my pack, three books by George Bowering.

                Queen Elizabeth Theatre—
        red-faced sleepers, torn bags and cardboard gone,
                the planters filled with magenta flowers—
they'd pitched a tent, for shiny new Mercedes
        and some vintage ones out front—
                the opera fund-raiser.

Down the sky-train steps—how heavy the books—
                no one was buying tickets. Sky train,
        the Japanese tourist said, last night. He had no other
                English, except Excuse me.

        Down the steps to Pender Lake
and the picket pickers and the man and the starlings—
        where *is* the train to the sky?

Coast Starlight

C.N. Station

Bus to Seattle sitting, waiting,
hatches up to the luggage bays.
Stooped hobbling man,
shaking with Parkinson's
grips a bag, two hands in the handle,
heaves it into lower compartment.

Lookit that ol' man, he's okay
yells a beggar,
torn shirt and grubby jeans,
grey stubble in the red cheeks,
rushing past a woman
hugging her friend goodbye—
why can't I do it, why can't I get
a couple of bucks for helpin' out?

U.S. driver watches,
silent.
The bags are loaded. People are loaded.
Parkinson's offers him a silver cigarette case.
Shows him how lights flash
red and blue when he flicks
a silver lighter. Why's this section
not open, he says.
Air conditioning units.
Driver looks down the platform
to wall-size grafitto on a warehouse—
R.S.B. dot dot dot.

Then closes hatches. Well, see ya tomorrow,
he says to his volunteer baggage loader.

Thoughts Leaving Richmond

would-be warehouses'
concrete walls standing roofless,

empty-windowed in fields
thoughts shoot through a tunnel

to a boathouse on a mirrored river,
journey outward, as in universe

pass a tractor in a field and a cultivator
or harrower—parked in pale dust

scored ridges—what is harrowed
then pylons carrying electricity—

high-tension wires on three tiers of arms
holding buckets

sentences, acres of glass houses, overheating
the mind—Asian lady moving to the sunny side

of the bus—U.S.A. University, her handbag saying—
Birch Bay—the tide is out leaving sand flats—mud sog—

crow landing in marshland—not rows in a field—
not dust but dark with humus and seedlings

Fraser River from the Bus to Seattle

Log booms' floating mats of tree stalks
squared off along the river banks.
Lumber-mills. Piles of beams and boards,
golden in the morning sun,
green forests turned to gold—
sitting stacked,
now that free-trade U.S. put a duty on it.

Lookit all those pallets
piled up around that factory.
Feeling like lots—
lots of something
when we hear only a few
can have plenty.

What is there lots of, anyway?
Air. Not clean air, but air.
Leaves of trees—of grass.
If you live here. Not in the Sahara.
Or the Gobi. Or the shanty towns
of Mexico City.
Cars. There's a lotta those.
Only to look at though—
not to *have*.

Thoughts are different—
you can talk in your head
as much as you like.
Don't drift too far on your river, though,
and forget you're operating a meat-slicer
or a plank saw.

Pacific Northwest

Seattle bus—six a.m.
From my window—
man on a railway track
no train in sight. Sawmill
vomiting brown sludge
from a long arm
over the yard. Bark chunks
a yard full.
And bull rushes
bent over a river in silver-green strips.
Home Depot Wal-Mart
their empty black-top roads
running through weedy lots
white arrows pointing left, right
white lines to stop
dotted down the middle of
new-laid edge-of-townness.
Trucks carrying logs—scabby
scraped. Scaling they call it
when you measure them.
As tho they were fish.
At a weigh station—lots and lots of wheels
of trucks rolling down the hill
back to the highway—
dinky toys.
Truck drivers, thru tiny windows
in their cabs. A Sikh in his turban.
A man in a ball cap slipping a cigarette
into his lips. A moustache—
gotta wrist watch, silver. Round face,
right hand holding C.B.—its spiral cord
from the top of the cab—whole life in a chair

with country slidin' by. Red motorcycle,
black rider. Pom pom—
size of a human head
sprung off a roof of a V.W. bug.
Then a field of small planes, snubnosed
yellow—where do they take off,
and fly. Sound Meat Distributors.
New world. Landscape.

Coast Starlight,

clackity clack down the track
words make rooms in our heads
rushing along
see a golf course, tiny bipeds
with tiny carts in the smooth
greens, then a sod farm's vast
perfect grass
for putting on with clubs
or putting on with gloves

Supreme Court bars
executing mentally retarded,
reports
the *Seattle Post Intelligencer*

Tacoma Bay

flat stillness spreading away to humps of trees and distant shore
in the foreground rotting pilings—what once were trees—
now splintered, barnacled, blackened by the sea
also a gym class—two groups of girls
red and blue—clustered on a long forever beach
no one else but a heron
and land sliding into sea
you see as weedy—
ducks floating over patches
the feeling of flat calm glass—
the blue of sky in green water
glistening on its surface
the tide rippling in—
end of a rotted jetty
old hulk, its stem curved into a sandbar—
look at it now, you see its back
is broken . . .

and who was Tacoma

Coming to Eugene

shunt engines
lumber cars, box cars, hoppers, tankers
perforated sides of live-stock cars—
can you stock life—
wet noses of terrified cattle
feathers of chickens bulging from cages
train call-call-calling our arrival

drink this way, says a long-haired dude
on a billboard
showing his milk-moustache

Eugene means "well born"—viz.
a couple of popes
and a French-come-Austrian general

or "well birth,"
says a midwifery conference ad

the first cabin erected in 1846
by Eugene Franklin Skinner
the town plotted out with Judge Risdon
settlers and industry arrived
a millrace
for flour mill, woollen mill, saw mills

lots of minutes, and even more seconds,
I think, for those who've not much else,
what or how do you *have*,
Kalapuya,
when they say have a nice day

Martinez 7 a.m.

immaculate brick station
super-clean concrete platform
ends at marshland—
sky overcast—just a dog barking
no one about except frogs,
straw-bleached hills dotted with pines
and the 1258 Southern Pacific steam-engine
fenced in long grass

in town, Bail Bonds America
red neon around a white star—
then Cooper Bail Bonds
Rick Calhoun owner agent
Contra Costa's oldest agency
established 1952
if agent is not in call 800-400-BAIL
NO COLLATERAL
LOW RATES (no surcharge)
CREDIT (upon approval)
STATEWIDE SERVICE (all jails)

30-foot scroll-top columns
hold-up for portico with pediment—
roof notched in imaginary beams
the County Finance Building
Latin *pedamentum*: a prop for a vine,
pedare: to furnish with feet

Supreme Court pediment in D.C.
robed men bearing scrolls, scales—
the temple of Zeus at Olympia, its horses
gods, goddesses

then the stone box of the county court house
shallow tiers of red brick steps
to five giant fluted columns
slapped over doors and windows
of California frontier

like on *L.A. Law*
if it has columns, it's justice

Pastime Club

level crossing
clang-clanging at the main drag
through Colfax—
U.S. Vice President 1869—
congressmen quietly receiving
undervalued shares in Crédit Mobilier
railway construction company
with profits of 23 million
just as debt-ridden Union Pacific
with same inside shareholders
uses up its government grant
("he denied the truth
of the charges brought against him")—

the town pride and joy
a North Western Pacific caboose
corralled in wrought iron pickets,
a row of brick blocks, peaked roofs
and false fronts—
Aimee's Attic Emporium,
the Railhead Saloon
Matilda's Classic Kitchen
with leaves and roses
on white-painted brick,
the Colfax Pharmacy—blue letters
over the boxed word DRUGS,
and the Pastime Club—
white letters on black signboard,
red edges jutting out
below PKG Liquors

Donner Summit

pulled out on the California Zephyr
pelicans in the marshland

mothball fleet, said our neighbour—
large paraffin balls, I thought,
what fantastic boats
suddenly in the misty grey bay
eight to ten flotillas
of U.S. Navy ships bundled up
rusting
in a sheet of glass

then up into red red earth
and lush green leaves
and further, to scrub-pine
in granite hills
pocked with scars of placer mines

Blue Canyon and Emigrant Gap
the route the Donners and Reeds took
oxen bolted—wagons, a hundred head of cattle
lost in the salt desert

train creaking like cart springs—
the struggle up
round the switch-backs
each heave of cross-tie
each shift in the rails—

"C'mon boys—as much land as you want
without costing you anything"

"Mrs. Murphy said
she thought
she would commence on Milt
and eat him.
I don't think she
has done so
yet"

Don't get side-tracked

Lunch yesterday—He
a figurative-drawing teacher
just retired not sure what to do
She still working—They
out on a jaunt to Portland
escaping kids and work
a little break at the Benson Hotel

Dinner—He
over-the-belt belly, long hair
said he was retired
(from growing pot may be)
been up north of Port Hardy
scuba diving—
normal's a word that's
never been applied to me
he said—
She
blousy hair, California drawl,
all smiles—They
had three sons including twins
all in their 20s—the twins
were locksmiths, the older son
a sawmill worker

Breakfast today—He
part-time electrical worker 59
likes to be out with the men
finds retirement tricky—She
former insurance secretary
teaches computer skills
at seniors' centres

people in a metal snake
chug-chugging the world

Lunch—the train jolts, stops—
lights, kitchens, air-coolers shut down—
sweltering Colorado heat oozes in
on a siding next to coal hoppers—We
play three-to-thirteen passing the time—
enthuse about the U.S. history
we're learning from the P.A. system—
They
from Milwaukee say
we have been here for 2000 years
since Christ was born
and before that we just don't know.

Nevada

country opens up—
dry dirt hills
dusted with creosote and sage—
the great basin where
the Humboldt river goes
to the Humboldt Sink
and the Carson River
goes to the Carson Sink

new-towns, suburban and treeless,
clusters of fuel silos, tin sheds,
abandoned concrete,
trailer encampments—a ladder of cross-ties
disappearing in the point
of converging rails, platforms,
telephone poles

flatness as wide as the eye can see
sand, silt dotted in windblown clumps—
alongside the train, wires
slicing the sky and distant hazed ridges

Harrah's hotel, Reno—
grey megalith 30 storeys up
to white clouds on blue—
lots more down town
festooned with gold

El Dorado, Holiday Inn,
the Sands, King's Head
signs for Crystal Ice and Oil

then yards of forklifts and cement trucks,
and row on row of storage lockers

Slow Down, a billboard says,
Gas Up

Porridge

breakfast, lunch, dinner
across the linen cloth
from Karen and Jim, Betty and Bob,
Susan and John, carnations in their vases
at each table—valleys, mountains,
lakes, rivers, trees, rocks, deserts
whizzing by our plates of small-talk Asian Stir Fry
or B.B.Q. Chicken Salad

now that I have a life—I've got friends
and a boyfriend—I don't write so much,
said the young daughter from the compartment
across the passage—all agog to find Peter and I
were writers—sat wide-eyed at our feet, we
tried to tell her what we did—
I like writing letters and in my journal,
she said—Peter told her about *Fidget*
and I about *A Thousand Mornings*—
yeah, said her dad, when she was little
I read her all the Disney stories

breakfast—I order potato grits—
the waiter brings just grits
like cream of wheat
only it's corn—

porridge, I said—

never heard it called porridge,
he said

Only the dreamings were original

Utah flat-tops

crumbling
layered cliffs
eaten away by rivers, streams

piles of scree fanned out around them
silted, hardened,
again eaten away

onto the flat seared plain

how to call these

bare eroded hummocks

leathery earth-size dragon-backs
eoned   skin

we reach the continental divide

not night visions, but ancestral beings
the cough-dreaming, the itchiness-dreaming
the dead-body-dreaming

how to call them

Helper, Utah

Carbon County in Mormon country
Pratt's Siding till 1892
brick townscape—sun-bleached—
false fronts
the crumbling hills, sparse sage—
satellite dish, pick-up trucks, a stop sign
in sharp-angled shadows

1990 pop.: two thousand, one hundred, forty-eight
1998: down by fifty-four—two thousand, ninety-four
the year Leo Steinbach at 90
(he found them developing dyes at Krakow)
still popped the occasional V
see the mining and railway museum,
Old Helper Hotel

Doctor, please, Mick Jagger said,
some more of these—
tongue lolling from high-gloss lips
Help me if you can,
a Beatle sang

coal-mining, livestock, and farms

in the land of gold,
Hinton Rowan H said
there'll be a *total absence*
of all the swarthy
and inferior
races

Across a divide

dark, 10:40 p.m.
Denver city spread out below—
rows and rows of lights
dots, pinpricks
a valley-full

we jolt—stop—
move—wait—
at a siding

produce our polishing,
to blithely serve our seat mates
agreeable opinions
we think they'll like

thru nightyards of silent machinery
backhoes, boxcars, trucks—
silently rolling into Denver—
arc lights over parking lots
half-lit fuel-silos
next to sidings of tanker cars—
bumping over switches
past containers labeled sealand,
hoppers of glinting coal
a mile of them, black hills
above our windows

our lives performed
for pleasing, for politesse
waiting till they can be instead
real—and alone
more silos and ducts,

gasworks, shadowed ribbing
the side of an arc-lit boxcar,
the man at dinner a tile-setter
and golfer—a Chicago man—
liked his son—took him camping—
took him to Yellowstone to see the geysers—
simple philosophy—my dad did it for me
now it's my turn—in his tie-dyed shirt,
drinking Pepsi

drift past another storage tank
for oil or gas—who knows—
under the concrete pilings of the freeway
pipes jut here and there from barren
ground—we jolt—stop
at another siding
hoppers, flatcars, boxcars sliding by
the things I edit out—my anger
despair, boredom
gas stations, hotels, feeder ramps
men carry torches between the tracks
fanning out every which way

halt—wait
for another thought
you only have to turn on your mind
to have something to do,
the retired electrician said
of Peter's writing

a transcontinental journey
across a divide—

it never seeming a country at war
backing into another line
shunting under a concrete ramp
over an underpass streaming cars
to where warehouses supply light bulbs
rich strikes in the boom city
of bonanza kings

Grand Junction Fruit Stand

passengers mill
in thick white heat
a table of green grapes,
oranges, watermelon,
bowls of dripping apples

so many photographs
seen but cut
before pointing the camera

in a horror story
the reader reads to have revealed
the brains
dished onto the plate

then the vampire killed,
the haunted exorcised

Arriving Reno

we're arriving Reno,
the conductor says,
our presence doing something
to Reno
itself a verb in the infinitive,
Harrah's fortress over the town—
the only living thing
the grey tipped wings
of a single gull
on a lamp post
above the green
waste-management skips

well gull, how do humans mean?

hot pink stucco hotels,
the star-spangled Comstock
the giant orange flames
licking the walls of the Phoenix

and Reno's gold glittered arch
for syntax

Ice-cream

Martinez platform—a hundred degrees.
Parked trolley and bags, hoisted day-packs
headed out to the town—accosted by Pat
from breakfast—sweet woman with no voice—
it's the canned air for three days, she whispered—
traveling coach class from Dallas.
Had to get a bus from Martinez to Napa.
To go cycling. Thirty miles a day, she said.
Slender limbs, kind eyes and smile
didn't look like they could do even five.

We told bathroom stories
over breakfast with Jim from Colorado—
yeah, I wuz from California
but I had to get out cuz of
the immigrant problem—I'm not
prejudiced or anything, he said—
Mexicans have a lower standard of living—
they like living in garages cuz
they're so much better than adobe huts.

Pat, catching us outside the station,
wanted us all to go for ice-cream
till her bus came.
There's a diner right by the station,
I said. We trudge over.
Closed Sundays.
Continue up the boiling street
past a rowdy bar.
Pat touches a tall tanned man
on the arm—standing outside the fence
around sidewalk tables.

Yeah, there's a one-way street
two blocks that way—
you'll find a convenience store.

Breakfast with Jim from sleeper class—
stories of shit-splattering
train toilets, and holes in the floor
of European bars.
With footprints on each side, he said.
A big lumpy man—shoulders
like a quarterback. Forearms still muscular
in his late 70s, but flesh of his chest
flopped about in loose boulders.
All I eat's fruit and meat,
he said, over a bowl of watery oatmeal—carbs
just turn into sugar and sugar turns to fat.

The town deserted—antique shops,
bail bond places all shut—
over there, Pat said, that looks like it—
we head off in another direction
drenched in sweat. A pizza place
sends us the opposite way—
zigzagging through brick and glass
and street grit.

Pat went back for her bus.
She'd worked for the Peace Corps
in Haiti—giving out food—
in the miles of shanty towns—
no schools, no hospitals, no roads—
dusty, naked kids digging holes in the ground

for a bucket of water—
till she had a nervous breakdown.

We double back—to search again
for the one-way-street convenience store
across gravel, concrete parking lot—
cracks running up a stucco wall—
aluminum windows and busted screen door
to chips, chocolate bars, tabloids, pop—

with ice-cream bar and broken popsicle
head back to our station.

Waiting for Coast Starlight

Trudge back to that place we saw
in hot concrete, deserted asphalt streets—
Louie Bertola's Family Style Dinners—
white railings up some front steps to a porch,
a yellow clapboard house, gingerbread trim—
the writer has no theory of the real but
opens the door to cavernous room,
ceiling fans, a shadowy bar—
something much harder.

Hesitate. No air-conditioning. Oh, what the hell!
The thing we'd share would be the word—
12 Formica tables, a vast open space, then a bar
with thick-topped stools, television, the ball-game on.
All complete dinners include soup, salad, pasta,
hot baked bread, and fresh sautéed vegetables.

Like theatre in the round
or bathing in the nude,
the writer orders a beer in the real—
Menu:
steak, calamari steak, pot roast,
grilled eggplant, chicken,
fish when available.

Without guns,
how do you talk about the real?
Two teenage girls, in light from blinded windows,
carry trays steaming from the basement kitchen.

Cash only—
no checks or credit cards in real.

The writer's trousers stick to his legs
in love with some blasted concept.

Get real, man. Tee-shirts, tattoos, black fingernails—
sitting across from frills and heels.
Shorts, running shoes—
white towels strapped to waists—two men
heaping dirty dishes, knives, forks
in grey tubs on the floor.

In the writer's head is a real.
Reader, do you see it?
Minestrone
in a battered steel bowl—
serve with plastic cook-spoon—
chunks of onion and cabbage
and conch-shell pasta.
Salad equals lettuce, carrot
and too much salad dressing.

We'd share the word—the thing itself—
battered eggplant—bludgeoned—coated—
with spaghetti. We'd chew the fibrous chard
and heap parmesan from a red plastic tumbler
onto the pasta.
It would be fine.
It would be real.

In the parlour car

people doing crosswords,
drinking beer, wine,
swiveling armchairs
at passing mountains
you're a judge
we don't talk about it
you said it had four letters
the closing words on the wounds
immune to corruption
what else is new
a hammer that's hard
the word is snitch
Minneapolis
Boston, Las Vegas
she was no nonsense
seven letters makes waves
it's been stacked for years
the Bureau, I mean culture
from a legal standpoint
overseas
our people go and kill everybody
and his mother and his dog
drug dealers killing us
Constitution has to come right out—
Supreme Court—our agencies—
how can you not racially profile!

Coast Starlight

the lighting under the edge
of the coast
where North America's a rug
and you can lift it
and see what's swept under
as in
her majesty

the lamps of reverie
nodding in lounge cars
on the trains of thought—
like it or not,
you're going to get caught

under the rug
in a velvet mantle
pinpricked
with glimmerings

Notes

Thanksgiving:
the Nevsky: broad avenue that leads into the large square in St Petersburg, scene of the February 1917 bread protests that started the Russian revolution (Carroll Terrell, *Companion to the Cantos*, re Canto 16 and Canto 74).

get the people out in the streets . . . : 1917 bread riots; Ezra Pound's source and mine is Lincoln Steffens, *Autobiography*, 750–51.

brush knee, fair lady works shuttles: tai chi moves. Fair Lady Works Shuttles is also called Four Corners.

"What is the meaning of this aggregation of filth"; "DEATH to 'merican freedom"; "I'll not permit a running sore to fasten itself . . ." : statements attributed to Captain Raymur (Tom Snyders, *Namely Vancouver*; JS. Matthews, Vancouver's first archivist; and R. A. J. McDonald, *Making Vancouver*).

law against Chinese washermen: a City by-law,1893 said Chinese laundries could only operate in two-block area between Carrall, Columbia, Hastings and Pender (Snyders).

What you see
Georgia, Richards, Burrard, Arbutus, Balsam, Larch, Trafalgar, Balaclava, Trutch, Blenheim, and Waterloo: Vancouver streets; all except the first three are in the Point Grey district, named after Captain George Grey. The Squamish called this area *Ulksen*, the nose.

Albert Norton Richards: a lawyer from Upper Canada, who used his liberal connections in Ottawa to gain appointment as Lieutenant Governor of B.C.

Sir Harry Burrard-Neale: an M.P. for Lymington and a navy pal of George Vancouver's. Burrard Inlet and Burrard Bridge in Vancouver are named after him.

Archibald Menzies: a botanist and surgeon on board George Vancouver's ship, the *Discovery*. George Bowering in *Burning*

Water, has Vancouver call him a porridge eater (he was a Scotsman). He spent time in Nootka Sound.

Arbutus menziesii: J. Pojar and A. Mackinnon, in *Plants of Coastal BC,* include the Straits Salish myth of Pitch, who "used to go fishing before the sun rose, and then retire to the shade before it became strong. One day he was late and had just reached the beach when he melted. Other people rushed to share him. Douglas-fir arrived first and secured most of the pitch . . ."

Sixteenth Earl of Derby: Frederick Arthur Stanley (Stanley Park) was Gov Gen of Canada 1888–93, Secretary of the Treasury 1877–78, and secretary for war 1878–80.

Horatio Nelson: won the battle of Trafalgar, but said at the beginning of the fight as he hoisted the signal "England expects that every man will do his duty."

Skwayoos: Squamish name for what is now known as Kitsilano Point.

Sens, Chelxwàelch, Pàpiyeq: Stó:lō place-names around Stanley Park (see *A Stó:lō Coast Salish Historical Atlas*).

Tatlow, Trutch: streets in Vancouver. Joseph Trutch was an engineer who built roads. He created some of the first reserves for First Nations people, but like others of his day ignored their claims to ownership. He was B.C.'s first Lieutenant Governor and according to the Encyclopedia of British Columbia "was a leading critic of responsible government—the principle that cabinet is accountable to an elected legislature—and resisted attempts to democratize government."

Connaught and Strathearn: Arthur William Patrick Albert, First Duke of Connaught and Strathearn, was made Govenor General of Canada 1895, nominally commander in chief of Canadian militia. He thought this meant he was really commander and kept interfering with the minister of militia in WWI, Sam Hughes.

Jerricho: name of a park on Vancouver's English Bay, and name of a military garrison in Vancouver. See also the *Book of Joshua* 6:21 & 24 and "Joshua," the song: "and the walls came tumbling down."

Walk for beans

Stolypin: In what passed for Parliament in Tsarist Russia, Peter Stolypin
brought in land reforms that severely disabled peasants. Many had
no horse even to till the land. Major uprisings occurred in 1905.
The "agrarian question" had to do with Stolypin's reforms regard-
ing peasant access to land so that they could subsistence farm,
which steadily reduced their ability to do this and provided no
infrastructure of education or equipment to overcome their starva-
tion conditions. Vladimir Kokovtsov followed Stolypin in 1911.

shacks floats tents . . . Prior Street Jungle: dispossession and housing
problems in Vancouver from the 1880s to 1930s (see Working
Lives Collective, *Working Lives*; Jill Wade, *Houses for All*).

the rain came down in sheets: J. S. Matthews, in *Early Vancouver*, Vol.
1, records this report of Colonel R. D. Williams, who looked up
from his desk at the Vancouver Harbour Commission one day to
find thirteen men trying to shelter under some rails.

Rosa Pryor: came to Vancouver in 1917 and, with no money, started a
fried chicken eatery. See Daphne Marlatt and Carole Itter, *Opening
Doors*.

Seymour: governor of the mainland B.C. colony in 1864 and governor
of the united colony in 1866. Margaret Ormsby notes Frederick
Seymour's description of Victoria as "a half alien, restless popula-
tion, ill at ease with itself." During his reign, the question of where
the capital of B.C. should be located was hotly debated. Ormsby
notes that Seymour was "a frail, slight man, completely bald" and
suggests that he probably saw "the imperial stump field" of New
Westminster as it was described by another British traveller: "at the
end of any vista nothing but sky and water and the eternal and
interminable timber." Seymour recorded that "the stumps and logs
of fallen trees blocked up most of the streets" (Ormsby). He dis-
covered that the courthouse "consisted of one small room in a
wooden building which had a canvas ceiling," and other privations
in public buildings. A man who enjoyed high living, he announced
"extensive improvements . . . to Government House in order to
provide it with 'a spacious and handsome ballroom, capable of
accommodating with ease two hundred dancers . . . supper rooms,
elegantly and substantially furnished apartments'"(Ormsby).

Royal City: A.K.A. New Westminster, first capital of mainland B.C.

khupkhahpay'ay: Squamish word for Cedar Tree (*Vancouver: A Visual Atlas*, Bruce Macdonald).

sold land to Crease: see Bruce Macdonald for land transactions.

Israel Wood Powell: see Chris Bracken, *The Potlatch Papers*. Powell Street runs along the waterfront in the industrial docks area.

Frances Street
Sister Frances (Frances Redmond): deaconess and founder with Father Fiennes-Clinton (under the auspices of St. James Anglican church) of St. Luke's Home, an early hospital in the poorest part of the city of Vancouver (1888). She directed the Home from 1888 till her death in 1932.

The Earl of Aberdeen: Prime Minister of Britain 1852–6 during the Crimean War (1854–5). Lord Russell and Lord Palmerston were in his cabinet—both strong-minded hawks. Aberdeen, the dove, couldn't control them.

Dunsmuir, Robert and *James* (father and son): British Columbia coal barons. Both also served as premiers of British Columbia.

Crimean War: ostensibly over control of religious sites in Palestine, but really over "the unresolved eastern question" i.e. western powers did not want Russia to dominate.

Palmerston: British statesman from the 1830s to the 1860s. Extremely outspoken, imperious foreign minister, regarded by the Queen as dangerous. Defence of the Ottoman empire was the object of his policy, with the goal of preventing Russia establishing herself on the Bosporus and preventing France establishing herself on the Nile. Palmerston acted against Egypt by organizing the northern powers and bombarding Beirut to cause the total collapse of the Egyptian leader Mehemet Ali. By 1840 his policies had terrified Europe. The French were ready to take arms. He squashed the intrigues of Afghanistan, trounced China at Chusan and bagged Hong Kong. He was turfed out of office in 1841 but got back in 1846. By 1848 he had alienated every other European power. Taking up the case of a British Jew David Pacifico whose house had been burned in an anti-Semitic riot in Greece, he gave his five-hour speech in the House of Lords demanding war against Greece. "Civis Romanus sum"—a British subject everywhere ought to be protected by the strong arm of the British government against injustice and wrong. After Aberdeen's government fell over the atrocities of the Crimean War, Palmerston was made Prime Minister.

yellow flags: a sign of small pox in the 1890s

a large airy room . . . brandy: advice from George H. Fox, *Practical Treatise on Smallpox* (located in the Vancouver City Archives).

Barrack Hospital at Scutari: the mess Florence Nightingale cleaned up.

Settlement Act: concerned the E & N Railway owned and operated by the Dunsmuirs. It provided settlers could preempt 160 acre lots for up to four years but after that they had to deal with Dunsmuir. Strangely most applications were delayed until after the four-year period.

diakonos: root of the word Deaconess which is what Sister Frances was. Nightingale (Sister Frances's prototype) spent three months at the Deaconess Institute of Kaiserworth est. 1836, studying the system.

Dear Sir,/ Thank you very much . . . : Letter from Sister Frances 1889 to Mayor Oppenheimer.

the standard as to quantity is still to be undertaken . . . : Letter from City of Vancouver re rooming house on Frances St.

Battle of Balaclava: Crimean War.

C'est magnifique . . . : comment of French general Bosquet re the battle of Balaclava.

Grey Nuns: early order of French-Canadian nuns who operated out of Montreal.

Captain Knox: fought in the Battle of Quebec 1759. The British expeditionary force took the city. Knox preferred the hospitals run by French nuns to what the British provided.

the enemy relentlessly . . . : message from the French to Haig at Festubert (Kitchener was C in C).

she brought them "socks shirts knives": she being Florence Nightingale.

nursing work as follows: 1901 *St. Luke's Home Report*.

patient used to dig potatoes and vegetables . . . and the cases which follow: these are typhoid cases of the sort Sister Frances and her staff would have had to deal with.

there have been not quite so many cases . . . and quotations over the next few lines: *St Luke's Home* annual newsletter reports in various years.

Soimanov, Pennefeather, Pavlov: generals in the Crimean War.

Battle of Inkerman, Crimean War.

"See the Conquering Hero Comes"/ the Esquimalt and Nanaimo Railway . . . : headline celebrating the opening of Dunsmuir's E&N railway.

C. F. A. Voysey: architect 1857-1941. The rebuilt 1924 St. Luke's Home (still extant) is a Voysey-style building.

Coast Starlight
Coast Starlight: name of a train that runs down the west coast to Los Angeles.

Tacoma Bay
Tacoma: Salish for "Mountain that was god" (i.e. now Mt Rainier) or "the mountain that provided rain to the tribe."

Coming to Eugene
Kalapuya: the Kalapuya occupied the Willamette River valley for centuries.

Thanks
First off, I'd like to thank everyone at NeWest Press. Publishers perform essential midwifery in the birthing of book babies, and NeWest excels at this art. Special thanks go to my editor, Doug Barbour, who could write the bible of literary obstetric care. The pre-natal period is, of course, crucial to healthy babies. While "eating for two," authors need lots of roughage and raw materials. I can't thank Vancouver City Archives enough for their nutritious meals, and their considered support of my Frances Street project. Periodic ultrasound for healthy fetal heart rate was conducted by Dave McFadden. Thanks, Dave, for marvelous comments, nudges, and spell-checks. Without encouragement, a nine-month pregnancy can very easily degenerate into a 48-month or a 120-month ordeal. Thanks go to *Capilano Review*, *Prism* and *Bird Dog* who published some of the poems in this book; to Daphne Marlatt for bringing me and "Frances Street" into her class on Vancouver writers; to Jacqueline Turner who helped me to rediscover form; to Rachel Blau Duplessis for cheer and good tidings; to Ezra Pound for blowing apart my syntax; and to Robin Blaser for being the blazing statue of liberty on the Columbia Picture screen of my world. And many, many thanks, incomparable thanks, to my husband Peter for companionship during breathing classes, knowing when to push and when not to push, and for constant support and encouragement.

At age eleven, MEREDITH QUARTERMAIN left her home in Toronto and drove with her family across Canada to the tiny, one-time silver boom community of Argenta, British Columbia. While living there she developed the strong sense of place that she carried with her throughout her studies at the University of British Columbia, and into every piece of writing since. In 1983 she was commissioned to write a history of York House School, thus beginning her exploration of Vancouver archival materials and pioneer narratives. Quartermain is the author of a number of books, and the founder of a literary web site called *The News* as well as the small literary press Nomados.